Literature written for young adults...

by young adults.

Allow yourself to be surprised.

The Eye of the Beholder

Young Writers Chapbook Series

Regan Nesbit

Press

Atlanta

Copyright © 2013 by Regan Nesbit
Published by VerbalEyze Press

All rights reserved. Printed in the United States of America. No part of this book may be used or reproduced in any manner whatsoever, including Internet usage, without written permission from VerbalEyze Press except in the case of brief quotations embodied in critical articles and reviews.

Cover artwork © 2013 by Susan Arauz Barnes
Editing by Derek Koehl and Tavares Stephens
ISBN: 978-0-9856451-2-0

VerbalEyze Press books are available at special discounts for bulk purchases in the United States by corporations, institutions and other organizations.

For information, address VerbalEyze Press, 1376 Fairbanks Street SW, Atlanta, Georgia 30310.

VerbalEyze does not participate, endorse, or have any authority or responsibility concerning private correspondence between our authors and the public. All mail addressed to authors are forwarded, but the publisher cannot, unless specifically instructed by the author, give out an address or phone number.

VerbalEyze Press
A division of VerbalEyze, Inc.
www.verbaleyze.org

Dedicated to Lizzie Mae.

Thank you for your wisdom and voice of reason
whenever I need something.
I love you with everything in me.

Table of Contents

Foreword 11
Editors' Note 13
Just Listen 15
Sorry 19
Truth 23
The Eye of the Beholder 25
Life 29
Love 33
Altered States 35
Scared of Lonely 39
Standardized Test 43
Mirrors 47

The Eye of the Beholder

Foreword

Many a black and white speckled notebook has been privy to the growing pains of young artists. They sketch, narrate, poet and rhyme to make sense of the world and orient themselves to the gravitational pull of coming of age. But their musings beg for answers and an empathetic head nod, so YaHeard? Poetics was born.

Whether speaking heartache at the mic, spitting social commentary over tracks or texting observations into the ether, the power and influence of word is undeniable and YaHeard? Poets study the craft, explore their creative process and learn how to promote their artistic endeavors through collaborations with organizations like VerbalEyze, a beacon for young artists.

YaHeard? was founded by Educator-Artists to support the creative stirrings of tweens and teens and the publication of this chapbook honors and encourages the work of a young artists whose passion and talent confirms them as part of a new generation of prolific writers, artists and musicians. Their musings have escaped from first notebooks and into your hands. Answer if you dare; head nod if you must ---this young scribe dares to explore the power of voice.

Ya Heard?

Susan Arauz Barnes
Co-founder, YaHeard? Poetics

Editors' Note

The Young Writers Chapbook Series is an expression of the mission and vision that is core to what we do at VerbalEyze. Through this series, we are able to provide talented, emerging young authors their debut introduction to the reading public. We are grateful that you also share an enthusiasm for young authors and the vibrant and energized perspectives they bring to our shared understanding of the human experience and what it means to live, love, long, lose and wonder as we travel together through this world.

We are pleased to bring to you an exceptional young writer, Regan Nesbit, with this edition of the Young Writers Chapbook. We trust that you will be as engaged and challenged by her words as we have been. Regan is part of an exceptional group of young writers, YaHeard? Poetics. She and her fellow writers are an never-ending encouragement and inspiration to us.

Read, enjoy and, as always, *allow yourself to be surprised*.

Derek Koehl
Tavares Stephens

Just Listen

Just listen

Stop talking

I'm trying to get out a sentence

I want you to understand

So sit back and listen

We need to get some things together

The sooner you listen, the better

Don't question until I finish

Because you'll be the first to witness

That I have a lot to say

If you would just listen

I have so many things in my head

Just waiting to be said

When I don't they come to mind

When I'm lying in my bed

So the things I left unsaid

Will now rise from the dead

And grace you with their presence

These words will be a present

Nothing I say I regret

The best part of the event

The look on your face when I finished

I wish I had a camera
Because that was just priceless
I slayed you with my words
So your eyes are now lifeless
And you shut your eyes their tightest
Out of all the times you've been quiet
I think this is the quietest
I guess you got the point
But what I'm really happy about
Is that you actually listened

Regan Nesbit

Sorry

I am sorry

Echoes in my head over and over

I am sorry

Becomes meaningless

I am sorry

Heard too many times before

I am sorry

Is it even the right word?

We've been through this too many times before

I say something

And you cut deeper

Now you want to apologize?

After this time what's going to happen?

I tried accepting the apologies

But you have put me down too long

I won't put up with it anymore

Sorry is so pointless

It never fixes what goes wrong

Sorry is overused

Played out

Cliché

Sorry is ineffective

I have no reaction towards it anymore

It's nonchalant

No emotion at all

You don't feel it

And I don't believe it

I'm sorry

You are sorry

A sorry excuse for breath

So keep your pathetic apology

Because I'm not accepting that

Regan Nesbit

Truth

Just tell me

Look into my eyes

The truth

Nothing more or less

I just want answers

The Eye of the Beholder

Written with Mariah Cooper

Blinded by the person they can only see

Beauty only comes with real personality

Made deaf by the compliments on just my looks

While I didn't take the time to realize what true beauty took

I don't know who I am only who I'm trying to be

Somebody who is not at all like me

But I'm supposed to please the people, right?

It's not like they can see the truth

Bumping right into the obvious clues

Because that girl lurking inside me

Doesn't like me or the person I'm trying to be

If only beauty wasn't a challenge I faced

Because the beauty I see is based on looks, body; race

You know if I was just a little lighter--maybe

They'd see my personality shines brighter--maybe

If my hair was less kinky

They would see that my hair doesn't define me

And if I didn't get such off-handed looks in so many places

Maybe people would see that I really could go places

They say beauty is in the eye of the beholder

Maybe I've given mine the cold shoulder
Maybe I can slide as perfect
But when they see me
I'm not worth it
All this time, effort that I put into looks
But they threaten my personality, creeping like crooks
Maybe if the world's attention was not wrapped up in blonde hair and blue eyes
You'd see that true beauty is where the soul lies
Because the look I have is more diverse
One of a kind in this universe
My skin should not land me in the pent house or the big house
Or inspire silence as quiet as a mouse
If you could see past a stereotype
You'd see my beauty is a rare type
I don't know the true definition of beauty
But I know where it starts
--With you
Because at the end you know
Who is truly beautiful

Life

The greatest show on earth

The things is there won't be five seconds 'til show time

No lines will be rehearsed

There is no script to get you back on track

Life is an improv session

We won't know what anyone says or comes up with

But you have to think quickly on your feet

When you get close to the resolution there will be no drum roll

When something goes wrong the background music can't warn you

You can't pretend to be a new character

—That would be lying to yourself

We all have roles in the show we're meant to portray

But in this show there are no small parts

Life is too big to be small

It doesn't really matter

Because once you're in the spotlight

There is no turning back

Because all eyes are on you

Some are waiting for you to fail

Some are waiting to see what you are made of

Just know you have to put on the greatest show on earth
Life

Regan Nesbit

Love

Love is confusing

But you can't live without it

An infinite drug

Altered States

I wish I knew

My mind is confused

That no means yes

So mixed

A scream is a hushed cry

A dream is reality

But is that really a bad thing

Unless a nightmare never gives me a scare

Something irrelevant becomes a care

Chasing becomes slow paced

Winning becomes last place

And what you want isn't worth the chase

How did I get in this state?

Every thought before is gone

But I knew self-confidence wouldn't last long

How do I doubt myself when others don't?

I try to deny it

But I won't

True we're our own worse critics

But I can't stand my own critiques

I don't realize what makes me unique

I guess you can say this is a phase

Hopefully all of this will change
Somehow I'll find a way
But I don't know
I never do

Scared of Lonely

I'm tired of pleasing everyone

Although I know why it's necessary

At the end of the day all you have

Is you

But if you're not pleasing them you end up alone

And something about being alone isn't right

I'm not ready for it yet

Still caught in the bliss of ignorance

Trying to understand my own adolescence

Not quite enough common sense

Pleasing becomes second sense

And I lose myself

Satisfaction the death me

Not physically but internally

I lose the things that make me

Me

I kill

Who I am

Making me someone else

A stranger in my mind

My own thoughts limited

I have no say over who I am anymore

All because the fear of being alone
I must risk solitude
For my own salvation

Regan Nesbit

Standardized Test

Okay class

Take your seats

Eyes on your own paper

If you don't have a pencil one will be provided for you

There will be no talking

Chewing gum

Getting up

Or leaving this class room

Keep your eyes on your own paper

If you need clarification on any question

Please raise your hand

Now open your test booklet and you may begin

What is this again?

Why do I even have to do this?

They're the same questions every spring

But I do my best

I am not going to be looked at as less

I'm tired of being judged by these tests

I mean it's that or you can look at me

Because I caught my teacher looking twice

Why does she have to look at me?

All I did was glance at my shoe

She does this to every kid sitting in my row
You know what?
Don't let it even get to you
Back to this test
Half this stuff we learned last year
And the other half we learned already
This test is a breeze
How do they expect us to learn anything new?
We have the same concepts every year
Just with a couple new words
It's not even challenging
I made sure I answered everything correctly
Because I refuse to be a test score
My name is not Scantron No. 882
That was not the name my mother gave me
I am a force to be reckoned with
I refuse to be unchallenged
I refuse to be a statistic
I refuse to be a standardized test

Regan Nesbit

Mirrors

Stand strong and face it

Being perfect is pointless

You are already worth it

 **Regan Nesbit** started writing when she was in the sixth grade during a semester of the school year spent focusing on poetry. It was a new experience for her but her Literate and Composition teacher, Mrs. Barnes, was very helpful to her and her classmates. At the end of the semester, Regan discovered a love for poetry and soon joined the YaHeard poetry group at her school. Joining the group helped her discover that music, and topics that get a rise out of her, inspire her to write.

Regan lives in Atlanta, Georgia with her mom and brother. She is now an eighth grader at the Ron Clark Academy, a middle school in southeast Atlanta. She enjoys hanging out with her friends, traveling with her school, and reading about the latest trends in fashion.

Photo credit: J. Amezqua

VerbalEyze Press

Empowering young writers to say, **"I am my scholarship!"**

Open call for submissions to the *Young Writers Anthology*!

See your work in print!

            Become a published writer!

                        Earn royalites that can help you pay for college!s

VerbalEyze Press is accepting submissions from young adult writers, ages 13 to 22, in any of the following genres:

- poetry
- short story
- songwriting
- playwriting
- graphic novel
- creative non-fiction

For submission details, visit
www.verbaleyze.org

VerbalEyze serves to foster, promote and support the development and professional growth of emerging young writers.

VerbalEyze is a nonprofit organization whose mission is to foster, promote and support the development and professional growth of emerging young writers.

The *Young Writers Anthology* is published as a service of VerbalEyze in furtherance of its goal to provide young writers with access to publishing opportunities that they otherwise would not have.

Fifty percent of the proceeds received from the sale of the *Young Writers Anthology* are paid to the authors in the form of scholarships to help them advance in their post-secondary education.

For more information about VerbalEyze and how you can become involved in its work with young writers, visit www.verbaleyze.org.

www.ingramcontent.com/pod-product-compliance
Lightning Source LLC
Chambersburg PA
CBHW022343040426
42449CB00006B/694